Torey Crust

See our other products!

THIS BOOK BELONGS TO

I SPY WITH MY LITTLE EYE, SOMETHING BEGINNING WITH...

A IS FOR

ACORN

I SPY WITH MY LITTLE EYE, SOMETHING BEGINNING WITH...

B IS FOR

BALE OF HAY

I SPY WITH MY LITTLE EYE, SOMETHING BEGINNING WITH...

I SPY WITH MY LITTLE EYE, SOMETHING BEGINNING WITH...

D

IS FOR

DECORATION

I SPY WITH MY LITTLE EYE, SOMETHING BEGINNING WITH...

E

IS FOR

EAR OF CORN

I SPY WITH MY LITTLE EYE, SOMETHING BEGINNING WITH...

F

IS FOR

FOX

I SPY WITH MY LITTLE EYE, SOMETHING BEGINNING WITH...

G

IS FOR

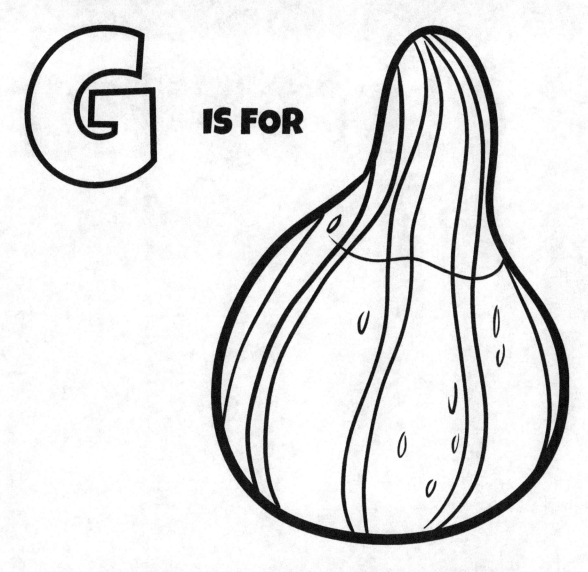

GOURD

I SPY WITH MY LITTLE EYE, SOMETHING BEGINNING WITH...

H

IS FOR

HAUNTED

I SPY WITH MY LITTLE EYE, SOMETHING BEGINNING WITH...

I IS FOR

ITCHY

I SPY WITH MY LITTLE EYE, SOMETHING BEGINNING WITH...

J IS FOR

JACKET

I SPY WITH MY LITTLE EYE, SOMETHING BEGINNING WITH...

K IS FOR

KNITTING

I SPY WITH MY LITTLE EYE, SOMETHING BEGINNING WITH...

L IS FOR

LEAVES

I SPY WITH MY LITTLE EYE, SOMETHING BEGINNING WITH...

M

IS FOR

MONSTER

I SPY WITH MY LITTLE EYE, SOMETHING BEGINNING WITH...

N

IS FOR

NAP

I SPY WITH MY LITTLE EYE, SOMETHING BEGINNING WITH...

O IS FOR

ORCHARD

I SPY WITH MY LITTLE EYE, SOMETHING BEGINNING WITH...

P

IS FOR

PUMPKIN PIE

I SPY WITH MY LITTLE EYE, SOMETHING BEGINNING WITH...

Q IS FOR

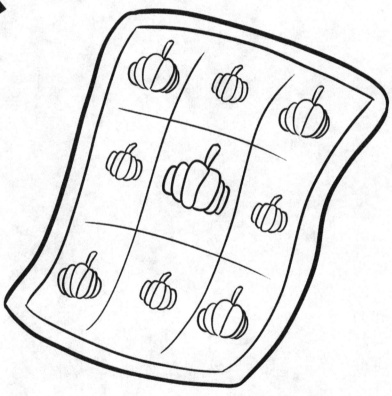

QUILT

I SPY WITH MY LITTLE EYE, SOMETHING BEGINNING WITH...

R IS FOR

RAKE

I SPY WITH MY LITTLE EYE, SOMETHING BEGINNING WITH...

S

IS FOR

SCARECROW

I SPY WITH MY LITTLE EYE, SOMETHING BEGINNING WITH...

T

IS FOR

TRUCK

I SPY WITH MY LITTLE EYE, SOMETHING BEGINNING WITH...

U IS FOR

UMBRELLA

I SPY WITH MY LITTLE EYE, SOMETHING BEGINNING WITH...

V

IS FOR

VOTE

VOTE

I SPY WITH MY LITTLE EYE, SOMETHING BEGINNING WITH...

W IS FOR

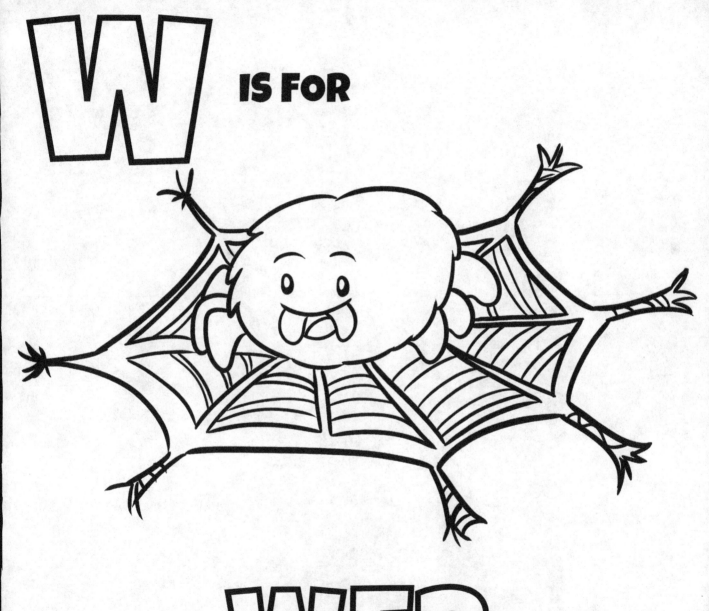

WEB

I SPY WITH MY LITTLE EYE, SOMETHING BEGINNING WITH...

X IS FOR

eXTRA LAYERS

I SPY WITH MY LITTLE EYE, SOMETHING BEGINNING WITH...

Y IS FOR

YAM

I SPY WITH MY LITTLE EYE, SOMETHING BEGINNING WITH...

Z

IS FOR

MAZE

One last thing...

We would love to hear your feedback about this book!

If you enjoyed this book or found it useful, we would be very grateful if you posted a short review on Amazon. Your support does make a difference and we read every review personally.

If you would like to leave a review, all you need to do is click the review link on this book's page on Amazon

Thank you for your support

Made in the USA
Columbia, SC
14 September 2023

22856101R00059